ADRENALIN!

Skateboarding

Clive Gifford

Chrysalis Children's Books

First published in the UK in 2005 by
Chrysalis Children's Books
An imprint of the Chrysalis Books Group Plc
The Chrysalis Building, Bramley Road,
London W10 6SP

ISBN 1 84458 403 8

British Library Cataloguing in Publication Data for this book is available from the British Library.

Associate Publisher Joyce Bentley
Senior editor Rasha Elsaeed
Project editors Jon Richards and Kate Simkins
Editorial assistant Camilla Lloyd
Designer Ed Simkins
Picture researcher Lorna Ainger
Consultant Chris Thomas
Chris has been skateboarding for over 18 years and has written for international and UK skateboarding magazines. He has travelled extensively around the world, visiting and trying out skating parks whenever he can.

Produced by Tall Tree Ltd, UK

Printed in China

10 9 8 7 6 5 4 3 2 1

Typography Natascha Frensch
Read Regular, READ SMALLCAPS and Read Space; European Community Design Registration 2003 and Copyright © Natascha Frensch 2001-2004 Read Medium, **Read Black** and *Read Slanted* Copyright © Natascha Frensch 2003-2004

READ™ is a revolutionary new typeface that will enhance children's understanding through clear, easily recognisable character shapes. With its evenly spaced and carefully designed characters, READ™ will help children at all stages to improve their literacy skills, and is ideal for young readers, reluctant readers and especially children with dyslexia.

Disclaimer
In preparation of this book all due care has been exercised with regard to the advice, activities and techniques depicted. The publishers regret that they can accept no liability for any loss or injury sustained. When learning a new sport it is important to get expert tuition and to follow any manufacturers' instructions.

Picture acknowledgments
All reasonable efforts have been made to ensure the reproduction of content has been done with the consent of copyright owners. If you are aware of any unintentional omissions please contact the publishers directly so that any necessary corrections may be made for future editions.
Alamy: Andersen-Ross/Brand-X 11t, Buzz Pictures 3, 4-5, Comstock Images 10, Kuttiq/Plain Picture 13t, Leo Sharp/S.I.N. 5, Emma Smith/Photofusion 28b, AP Photo: Kevork Djansezian 27t, Boulgakow: Quiksilver.com 29, Cover Corbis: Al Fuchs/NewSport 27b, Ted Soqui 9t, Keith Folken: 14, Getty Images: Evan Agostini 26, Harry How 1, 9b, 17l, 25b, 32, Jed Jacobsohn 12, Robert Mora 7t James Hudson: 13b, 15, 16, 17c, 18-19, 20-1, 22, 23, 24, 25t, 28t, Pete Knowles: 6, Charles Lillo: www.cgldesigns.com 8, Robert Opie: 7l

Contents

Street surfing

Skateboarding is one of the most popular street sports in the world, and with good reason – it's fast, challenging, exciting and action-packed. It's a sport that has also created its own styles of fashion and music.

A sport with no rules

All over the world, skaters enjoy the freedom that skateboarding gives them and their friends. Unless you are competing in official contests, there are no rules. Skateboarders have their own style, fashion, bands and culture that sets them apart from the rest. Skateboarding offers a constant challenge that many find addictive – and there is plenty to keep you hooked. As soon as you've nailed a tough trick, there is always another one to work on.

Skating words

'Sk8r' is short for 'skater'. Here are a few more skateboarding terms.

GNARLY	Fast and exciting.
GROMMET	A beginner.
JAM	A meeting of skateboarders for a skate session.
SICK	Very impressive trick or move.
SNAKE	Someone who pushes into a queue.
THRASH	To wear down your board through plenty of skating.

Street or vert

There are two main types of skateboarding – street and vert. Street involves riding around an urban environment using obstacles and street furniture, such as kerbs, handrails and stairs. Vert riding is performed on large ramps and bowls. It involves acrobatic twists, handstands and mid-air turns above the top edge or lip of the ramp or bowl.

One of the key moves in street skating is the boardslide, where the rider slides down an obstacle, such as a kerb or a rail, using the middle of the underside of the board.

5

The roots of skateboarding

Skateboarding began in California, USA, at the end of the 1950s. Surfers fitted wheels to strips of wood in order to 'surf' on the streets on days when there were no waves.

Riding the sidewalk

This early craze of skateboarding was dubbed 'sidewalk surfing'. Two big names in surfing – surf star Hobie Alter and the publisher of the *Surf Guide*, Larry Stevenson, started building skateboards. There was enormous interest and over 40 million skateboards were sold in just three years. However, many accidents occurred and cities started banning skateboards from their pavements.

A SURFER PASSES THE TIME SIDEWALK SURFING ON A CALIFORNIA STREET IN THE 1960S.

SKATING FACT

On 15 May 1998, Billy Copeland reached a record speed of 112 km/h thanks to his modified skateboard that was fitted with a cluster of rockets.

THIS SKATEBOARD FROM THE 1970S HAS A THINNER DECK AND THICKER WHEELS THAN TODAY'S MODELS.

The sensational seventies

The 1970s saw a whole range of boarding innovations. First, the kicktail, the upwards sloping tail of the board, was developed in 1971, allowing skaters to perform flips and wheelie tricks. Then urethane wheels were developed for skateboards. These created much better grip on the ground, allowing riders to perform even more stunts. Vert riding began to take over from cruising along streets as the most popular type of skateboarding. Skateboards changed, too, growing in width to give a wider, more stable platform for vert riding. The first skatepark was opened in Florida, USA, in 1976, and dozens more followed around the world.

Boarding booms

Throughout the 1980s and 1990s, skateboarding had more downs than ups. In the last decade, however, it has boomed thanks to increased exposure on TV, in films and at special events and competitions.

The Ollie

If one single move revolutionised skateboarding, then it has to be the Ollie, also known as the no-hands aerial. This trick was named after its inventor Alan 'Ollie' Gelfand, who was just 16 when he first nailed the move in 1978. The Ollie is a type of jump made without using the hands to lift both rider and board into the air. As word of this move got round, it allowed skateboarders to use kerbs, rails and benches as if they were ramps in skateparks.

INVENTOR OF THE OLLIE, ALAN GELFAND, WHO STARTED SKATING AT THE AGE OF 11.

Timeline

1963 First skateboard contest held at Pier Avenue School, California.

1973 Nasworthy's Cadillac urethane wheels go on sale for the first time.

1976 A concrete bowl in London becomes Europe's first skatepark.

1978 Alan Gelfand invents the Ollie.

1982 Tony Hawk wins his first competition at the Del Mar Skate Ranch.

1993 World Cup Skateboarding organisation formed.

1995 Skateboarding features at the ESPN Extreme Games.

2000 Skateboarding becomes the USA's sixth most popular sport.

California skating

Dogtown was the nickname of part of Venice, California, where a group of talented skateboarders, including Tony Alva, Jay Adams and Stacy Peralta, developed their own skating style in the late 1970s. Known as the Z-Boys, this group of skaters was immortalised on screen nearly 30 years later when the film *Dogtown and Z-Boys* (2001) was released.

TONY ALVA WAS ONE OF THE ORIGINAL Z-BOYS AND NOW RUNS HIS OWN COMPANY MAKING SKATEBOARDS AND SKATING CLOTHES.

SKATEBOARDING NOW PLAYS A CENTRAL ROLE IN X-GAMES EVENTS AROUND THE WORLD, WITH SKATERS REGULARLY PERFORMING IN FRONT OF THOUSANDS OF PEOPLE.

Back for good

During the lean years of the 1980s and 1990s, a hardcore following kept skateboarding alive. By the mid-1990s, a new crop of teenagers was getting into the sport. Skateboarding got lots of exposure on new television channels and over the internet. The ESPN Extreme Games, now called the X-Games, featured skateboarding from 1995 onwards and gave the sport huge TV coverage.

Skate gear

The most important part of any rider's kit is the board. Hundreds of different boards exist – get an experienced rider to help you choose one. Make sure the trucks are made of aluminium and that the truckbolts lie flat on the deck.

The tail is the back of the deck. It is turned upwards into what is called the kicktail. This is used to flick the front of the board up for tricks.

On the deck
The underside of the deck is sometimes finished with a smooth, shiny plastic to help riders slide the board over obstacles. If your deck has this finish, then it is called a slick. Boards without this are just referred to as wood boards.

Bearings are fitted inside the wheels to help them roll smoothly.

Deck check
Caring for your board will make it last longer and help you to perform at your peak.

- Make sure your board is clean and dry and that the grip tape isn't loose and flapping.
- Check that your truckbolts and wheel nuts are tight. If you can loosen them with your fingers, they are not tight enough.
- Wheels wear over time, particularly on their outer edge. Check your wheels for wear and turn them round to make them last longer.
- Check that the bearings inside the wheels are clean and greased so that your wheels run smoothly.

Trucks can be adjusted for tightness or looseness. Looser trucks make for easier turns.

Running smoothly

Good wheels tend to be made of a material called urethane. Small wheels (53 mm in diameter or smaller) are good for flipping skateboards and doing tricks. Larger wheels (56 mm and bigger) are used for cruising and vert riding. Trucks are made of aluminium and consist of the baseplate, which attaches to the board, and the hanger onto which the wheels are bolted. Heavyweight trucks are used by street skaters, who grind their trucks regularly.

CARRY A SET OF SPANNERS WITH YOU SO THAT YOU CAN TIGHTEN YOUR TRUCK AND AXLE BOLTS.

Grip tape covers some or all of the top of the deck and gives your feet extra grip.

The deck is made up of layers of wood that are bonded together.

Truckbolts fix the trucks to the deck.

The nose is the front of the board.

Skate style

Skateboarding has its own distinctive fashion. Some of the gear worn or carried is a matter of personal style, but other items, such as good shoes and a helmet, help you to skate well and safely.

A helmet should have a chinstrap to keep it from slipping.

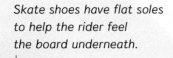
Skate shoes have flat soles to help the rider feel the board underneath.

Skater clothing

Skateboarders tend to wear loose-fitting clothing that doesn't restrict their movement. Long-sleeved T-shirts help to avoid grazes on arms from a fall. Long trousers also protect the legs from grazes. Trousers with zipped pockets will keep your money and keys safe when you get some air. Finally, special skate shoes made from tough materials with durable stitching can be bought.

WEARING THE CORRECT SAFETY GEAR IS IMPORTANT TO PREVENT SERIOUS INJURY.

SKATING FACT

In 2003, skaters spent a staggering US$5.7 billion on skateboards and gear in the USA alone!

Skatepark kit

A backpack holds all you need for a great day's skating – a water bottle, sunscreen, a top, a spanner and a camera to capture any cool moves. An old cloth is good to wipe your board down after a serious session.

SKATEBOARDERS AND IN-LINE SKATERS SHARE MANY OF THE SAME FASHIONS AND TRENDS, SUCH AS LOOSE T-SHIRTS AND BAGGY SHORTS.

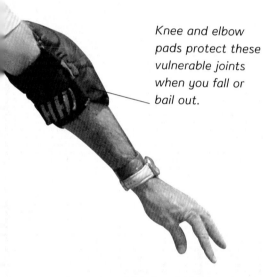

Knee and elbow pads protect these vulnerable joints when you fall or bail out.

Loud and proud

Skateboard manufacturers sell thousands of items of their clothing through both specialist skateboarding shops and high-street stores. Skateboarding clothes are usually covered with radical designs. Some groups of skateboarders get their own 'team' shirts printed.

SKATEBOARD BRANDING APPEARS ON T-SHIRTS, TROUSERS, SHOES AND OTHER EQUIPMENT.

Skateboard science

Scientific principles play an important part in the skateboarding experience. One of the most important principles is friction, which helps skaters perform tricks and stay on their board.

A SKATER APPLIES GRIP TAPE TO THE TOP OF HIS DECK. GRIP TAPE COMES IN PRE-CUT SHEETS WITH A ROUGH TOP SURFACE TO INCREASE FRICTION AND GRIP.

Gripping stuff

Most people understand that friction slows you down. It provides the necessary grip, called traction, that allows people to stand and walk. If you didn't have friction, you would skid and slide all over the place. The soles of skate shoes and grip tape on top of the deck increase friction to give you the extra grip necessary to stay on your board as you perform a move. Friction also helps your skateboard's wheels grip the road so that they move your skateboard forwards as they turn.

SKATING FACT

The Exkate X-24 electric skateboard went on sale in 2004 in the USA for a cool US$999 (UK£555). Controlled by a wireless remote, the skateboard can accelerate from 0 to 35 km/h in just four seconds!

Balls and bearings

Friction slows movement down, and extra energy is required to overcome it. Skateboard designers look to reduce friction between the wheels and the axles on which the wheels turn. They do this by using a lubricant, such as oil or a fine powder, and by using devices called bearings. A bearing is a ring containing lots of small steel balls. It sits between the skateboard wheel and the axle.

THE BALLS IN THE BEARINGS CONSTANTLY ROLL OFF THE AXLE, GIVING A SKATEBOARDER A SMOOTH RIDE.

A-grade

The hardness of skateboard wheels is measured by an instrument called a durometer. Skateboard wheels are given an 'A' rating from a durometer – usually between 90 and 100. The bigger the number, the harder the wheel. A softer wheel will flatten during a ride to give more grip but less speed.

MOST STREET AND VERT SKATERS CHOOSE WHEELS WITH AN 'A' RATING OF 96–98. SOFTER WHEELS, WITH A RATING OF 75–90, ARE USED ON ROUGHER TERRAIN, SUCH AS CRUISING ON ROADS.

Gravity games

It's not just skateboard kit that relies on science to work. Skateboarding moves work because of scientific forces, such as gravity.

JUST BEFORE DROPPING INTO A HALFPIPE, A SKATER CLAMPS THE BOARD TO THE RIM USING THE REAR FOOT.

Dropping in

Skaters sometimes enter a halfpipe from the top and not the bottom, using a technique called dropping in. They stand at the top of the ramp with their board jutting out over the edge. As they lean forwards on the board, the gravity takes over. Gravity is the pulling force that draws things towards the Earth's surface. Gravity pulls the front of the rider's skateboard downwards, where its wheels meet the surface of the halfpipe.

SKATING FACT

On 17 April 2002, Danny Way from the USA broke the record for the highest air on a skateboard. He soared to a jaw-dropping height of 5.56 m above the lip of a halfpipe!

Pumping principles

Skateboarders build up speed in a halfpipe by using a technique called pumping. When on the bottom part of the pipe they crouch down. As they rise up the slope of the pipe, they straighten their legs. This technique works because the riders are shifting their centre of mass, the point where the entire weight of the rider's body is balanced.

SOME COMPETITIONS SEE SKATERS ATTEMPTING TO GET THE MOST HEIGHT, OR AIR, ABOVE THE RIM OF THE HALFPIPE.

AT THE BOTTOM OF THE HALFPIPE, THE SKATER SHOULD BE FULLY CROUCHED DOWN.

Above and beyond

By raising their height as they ride upwards, skaters are increasing the energy in their movement. This means that they increase their speed. A serious pumping session will get a skater up and beyond the top of the halfpipe.

Skating moves

You've got your board and you want to start moving. However, first you need to check out your stance and pick the one that most suits you.

R U goofy?

Your feet should be nicely spread on the board – aim for your feet to cover the truckbolts. There are two stances – regular (with your left foot forwards) or goofy (with your right foot forwards). Try out each stance to see which feels most natural to you. Don't worry if you're a goofy as you're in good company – skating legend Tony Hawk also skates goofy.

THIS SKATER IS RIDING WITH A GOOFY STANCE.

Starting

Don't be a mongo foot! This is when you leave your back foot on the board and push off with your front foot. Instead, leave your front foot on to guide the board. Your back foot leaves the board to paddle the ground smoothly to build up a little speed. Once you have pushed off, get your back foot on the board and try to stay balanced.

Stopping

At first, just try to stay on the board until it stops. The easiest way to stop is to drag your back foot along the ground. The extra friction created between your shoe and the ground will slow the board down. Alternatively, and to save wearing out your trainers, your back foot can be used to run alongside the board.

MASTERING HOW TO STOP THE BOARD IS JUST AS IMPORTANT AS LEARNING HOW TO GET IT MOVING.

Frontside turns

The simplest turning moves involve keeping your feet on the board and the wheels on the ground. It's all about shifting your body to get your deck to veer off.

1. Choose a flat, empty place to begin. Push off to get you and your board moving.

2. Lean forwards gently and press down on the edge of the board with your toes.

3. You should feel the board veer to one side. You are now performing a frontside turn.

4. To complete the turn, put the weight back on the whole of your feet and your board will straighten up.

19

Turns and burns

Once you've nailed moving, stopping and simple turns, you can start to look at more radical moves. The tricks on this page are useful building blocks to the really spectacular pro moves.

Kickturns

Kickturns are very useful for changing direction quickly. Move your front foot to the middle of the board and your back foot to the rear. Press down gently on the back of your board and your deck's nose and front wheels should rise off the ground. As the wheels come off the ground, twist your body in the direction your heels are facing to skew the board around.

SKATING FACT

In 2000, Danny Wainright performed the highest Ollie off flat ground when he cleared 1.13 m!

AT THE END OF A KICKTURN, LEAN FORWARDS TO BRING THE FRONT WHEELS BACK DOWN TO THE GROUND.

Getting airborne

To perform an Ollie, you start from a crouched stance on your board with your front foot just behind the front truck. Push down hard on the tail of your board so that it touches the ground. At the same time, take the weight off your front foot. As the front starts to rise, drag your front foot along the board towards the nose and lift your back foot. You will now be airborne. Your board will start to level out in mid-air and then it's just a matter of keeping your balance.

OLLIES ARE USEFUL FOR JUMPING OVER SMALL OBJECTS AND FOR JUMPING ONTO RAILS, BENCHES AND OTHER STREET FURNITURE.

Heelflips and kickflips

Once you've mastered the Ollie, there are a whole host of related tricks that look spectacular, such as heelflips and kickflips. For a heelflip, set up as you would to do an Ollie but have your toe off the board a little. Kick down the tail as hard as you can and slide your front foot completely off the nose, flicking it with your heel to spin the board. As soon as it does a full flip, put both feet back on the board and land it once again. To perform a kickflip, do an Ollie and kick your foot to the heel side to spin the board.

THIS SKATER IS PERFORMING A SPECTACULAR KICKFLIP.

Skateboarding safety

Skateboarding can be dangerous. In the USA, around 50 000 riders are taken to hospital with skateboarding injuries every year. Many accidents can be avoided by wearing the right gear and skating in safe surroundings.

Protection

If you skateboard, you will fall. Fact. So it makes sense to protect the most vulnerable parts of your body. These are your knees, elbows and head. A helmet is a must. Modern helmets are lightweight and have a hard, outer shell and a soft, comfy layer inside. A padded chinstrap allows you to adjust the fit. Elbow and knee pads are also vital. A lot of skateboarders riding ramps wear wrist guards, which protect wrists from bending and breaking during a fall.

THESE SKATERS ARE KITTED OUT IN PROTECTIVE GEAR FOR A SESSION AT AN INDOOR PARK.

Bailing out

You will want to avoid as many slams – bad or unexpected crashes – as possible. Sometimes when you are out of control, the best thing is to jump off your board and try to land on your feet safely. Other situations call for a bailing out move. One of the most common is the roll. This sees you crouch low, step off the side of the board and perform a roll with your body as relaxed as possible. It's a natural reaction to stick out your hands on falling but try to avoid doing this, as it is the cause of the most common broken bones in skateboarding – wrist and lower arm.

BY FALLING TO YOUR KNEES IN A KNEESLIDE, THE PROTECTIVE PADS WILL ABSORB MOST OF THE FORCE.

Kneeslide

You should always wear knee pads when riding ramps and halfpipes. The reason is simple. If you want to bail out on a ramp, the best way is to fall to your knees, keeping them together, and slide down the ramp.

Fit to skate

Skateboarders rarely train like athletes in other sports. Instead, they spend as much time on their boards as possible, running through moves and honing tricks for hour after hour until they can nail a particular grind, turn or jump over and over again.

Stretch for success

Warming up helps to get the blood moving around your body. Good warming up moves are light jogging, stretching your legs and knee bends. Your legs, back and ankles take a lot of punishment when skateboarding. Stretching these parts of the body will enable you to skate longer and better and help cut down the chances of getting a muscle injury.

YOU SHOULD SPEND 15 TO 20 MINUTES WARMING UP BEFORE A LONG SESSION.

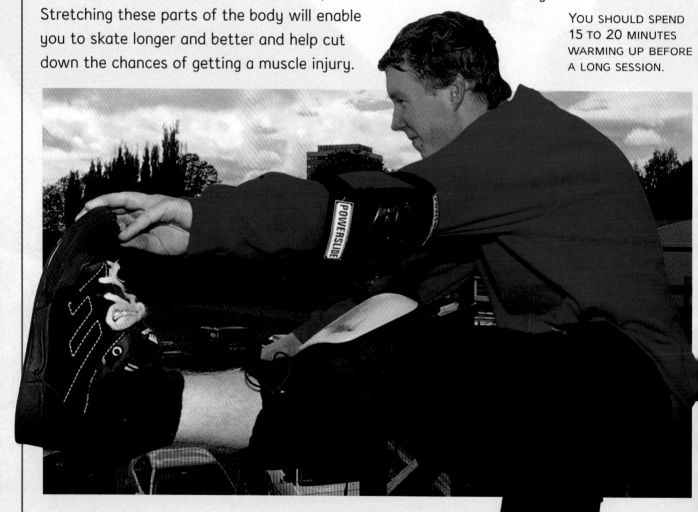

Practice makes perfect

Building up a full repertoire of tricks takes hours of constant practice. Spending time on your board is the only way you will be able to master the most complicated tricks.

FALLING OFF IS ALL PART OF THE LEARNING EXPERIENCE. THE BEST THING IS TO GET BACK ON YOUR BOARD AND KEEP TRYING.

Turning pro

The dream of many skateboarders is to join their heroes and become professional. Only a handful of incredibly talented and very dedicated riders can make it. The ladder to the top starts with local, regional and national competitions. The next stage is getting sponsorship from a local skateshop or even a major manufacturer. For the very best, the rewards are great. Their money comes from winnings and from sponsorship fees. Many riders for top skateboarding teams also earn a monthly salary.

PRO SKATEBOARDERS, SUCH AS TONY HAWK, MAKE THEIR MONEY FROM COMPETITIONS, DISPLAYS AND ENDORSING PRODUCTS, SUCH AS COMPUTER GAMES.

SKATING FACT

In his early career, Tony Hawk knocked out his front teeth three times!

Famous skaters

Skateboarding has made worldwide stars and celebrities of its very best riders. The top pros draw huge crowds when they go on tours around the world.

Tony Hawk

The Hawk is simply the most famous skateboarder. He first rode a hand-me-down skateboard from his elder brother, Steve, when he was 9. By the age of 12 he was already being sponsored. The most successful competition skateboarder, Hawk stunned crowds at the 1999 X-Games, where he became the first person to nail a 900 – two-and-a-half spins at the top of a ramp. Hawk founded the Birdhouse team, one of the world's leading skateboard outfits that includes top-class pro riders, such as Willy Santos and Bucky Lasek. Having retired from competition at the end of 1999, Hawk still skates at demonstrations and shows all around the world.

HAWK HAS WINS IN OVER 70 PRO SKATEBOARDING COMPETITIONS.

SKATING FACT

Tony Hawk has his house fitted with skate ramps outside and special floors inside, allowing him to skate around his house.

Vanessa Torres

Within four years of taking up skateboarding at the age of 13, Californian Vanessa Torres crowned a meteoric rise in the sport by winning gold at the 2003 X-Games. Two years earlier, she had destroyed the competition by winning every event she entered. A fast and aggressive rider, she is considered by many to be the future face of skateboarding.

Elissa Steamer

Born in Florida, USA, Elissa Steamer is one of the most famous female skaters around. She has been skateboarding since she was 12 and turned pro in 1998. She became the first female rider to have a pro model skateboard named after her.

IN SEPTEMBER 2004, ELISSA RODE TO VICTORY AT THE GRAVITY GAMES IN CLEVELAND, OHIO, USA.

Bob Burnquist

Bob was born and raised in Brazil, and he is famous for switchstance riding. This is riding a skateboard the opposite way to your normal stance.

BURNQUIST STARTED RIDING AT THE AGE OF 11.

BORN	Sao Paulo, Brazil, 1976
HEIGHT	188 cm
WEIGHT	75 kg
CAREER FACTS	Vert world champion, Bob Burnquist burst onto the scene at age 18, winning the 1995 Slam City Jam in Canada. In 2002, he won a Laureus World Sports Person of the Year award, which was presented to him by his hero, NBA basketball star Michael Jordan.

Great skating

Skateparks range from small, indoor locations with one or two wooden ramps to giant, outdoor parks with concrete bowls, halfpipes and street sections. Skating at a good skatepark is great fun and allows you to check out other skaters' moves.

Park furniture

A good skatepark has a range of different ramps and shapes to skate on, including kerb blocks that simulate a street kerb but let you slide and grind along either side. Small fly-off ramps allow you to get airborne and pull a trick in mid-air. Many skateboarder's favourites are the quarterpipe and the fun box – a rectangular platform with ramps on each of its four sides. Concrete bowls can be round or oval shaped. Some have long curves from side to side and are known as snake runs.

THIS FUN BOX HAS A RAIL FITTED TO ITS FAR SIDE FOR SKATERS TO GRIND ALONG.

Area 51 Skatepark

LOCATION Eindhoven, The Netherlands

DESCRIPTION A huge indoor arena, filled with fun boxes, ramps and halfpipes.

HISTORY Opened in July 2002.

ATTRACTIONS The park features Europe's largest skatebowl, the MU Bowl, as well as a massive street course, a kids' corner and a chillout area.

Marseilles skatepark

The best in France and arguably one of the best in the world, the Marseilles skatepark has a series of concrete bowls and lots of great riding lines. Home of the annual Bowlrider competition, its design has inspired a new skatepark in Vancouver, Canada.

SOARING ABOVE A BOWL AT THE MARSEILLES SKATEPARK.

American parks

The first skateparks were built in Florida in the mid-1970s, and the USA still leads the way with many of the world's best parks. One is the Burnside park in Portland, which was designed and built in 1990. This famous site featured in the best-selling *Tony Hawk Pro Skater* video game.

Skateboarding words

acid drop To ride straight off something and freefall to the ground.

air When skaters clear jumps or obstacles.

bailing out To leave your skateboard in order to avoid a major crash.

boardslide To slide on an obstacle, such as a kerb or a rail, using the middle of the underside of the board.

carves Wide turns with all four wheels in contact with the ground.

coping Metal piping or edging that has been fitted to the lip of a ramp or halfpipe to provide extra grip.

dropping in To enter a ramp or obstacle from the top.

fakie Riding backwards.

grind Scraping one or both axles on a kerb, railing or other surface.

grind box A block or box that has coping along its sides that allows skateboarders to perform grinds.

grip tape Self-sticking tape with a sandpaper-like finish. This is stuck to the deck of a skateboard to provide extra grip.

halfpipe A large U-shaped ramp of any size, which usually has a flat section in the middle.

heelflip A variation on the Ollie in which skaters spin the board using their heels.

kickflip A variation on the Ollie in which the skater kicks the board into a spin before landing back on it.

McTwist A 540-degree turn performed on a ramp. It is named after skateboarder Mike McGill.

Ollie A jump performed by tapping the tail of the board on the ground. It forms the basis of many skating tricks.

pumping Moving your bodyweight on the board to generate speed.

slam A hard, uncontrolled crash or fall from your board.

street skating Skating on streets, kerbs, benches and other street furniture.

truck The fitting on the underside of the board that holds the wheel axles.

urethane The special sort of plastic material used to make skateboard wheels.

vert ramp A ramp that has a vertical section at the top.

vert skating Skating on ramps and other vertical structures, such as halfpipes and quarterpipes.

Films

Dying To Live (2002)
An all-action movie from Zero skateboards, showing their pro skaters performing stacks of moves and tricks.

Transworld Skateboarding: Sight Unseen (2002)
Skateboarding as art, with a good mix of street skating styles.

Books

Skateboarder's Start-Up by Doug Werner (Tracks Publishing, 2000)
Radical Sports: Skateboarding by Andy Horsley (Heinemann, 2003)
Skateboarding: Book of Tricks by Steve Badillo and Doug Werner (Tracks Publishing, 2003)
Hawk: Occupation Skateboarder by Tony Hawk and Sean Mortimer (Harper Collins Willow, 2002)

Magazines

In the UK, *Sidewalk*, the successor to *R.A.D. skateboarding*, has been informing and entertaining skateboarders since 1995.

The US skateboarding scene is really vibrant, and long-running magazines like *Thrasher, Transworld Skateboarding, Slap* and *Skateboard Magazine* are available in bookstores and at skate shops. UK skateshops often import copies of these magazines.

In Australia, imported UK and US magazines are found in many skate shops. *Australian Skateboarding Magazine* is dedicated to the Australian boarding scene.

Index